The Silent Flute

The Silent Flute

Professor Arun Chandra Sahu

BLACK EAGLE BOOKS
Dublin, USA
Bhubaneswar, India

BLACK EAGLE BOOKS

USA address:
7464 Wisdom Lane
Dublin, OH 43016

India address:
E/312, Trident Galaxy, Kalinga Nagar,
Bhubaneswar-751003, Odisha, India

E-mail: info@blackeaglebooks.org
Website: www.blackeaglebooks.org

First International Edition Published by
BLACK EAGLE BOOKS, 2024

THE SILENT FLUTE
(A collection of English poems being transcreated by the author himself from his original Odia poetry collection 'Nishabda Banshiswana')
by **Prof. (Dr.)Arun Chandra Sahu**
Email: sahuac52@gmail.com

Copyright © **Professor Arun Chandra Sahu**

All rights reserved. No part of this publication may be reproduced, stored in a retrieval system, or transmitted, in any form or by any means, electronic, mechanical, photocopying, recording or otherwise without the prior permission of the publisher.

Cover & Interior Design: Ezy's Publication

ISBN- 978-1-64560-614-7 (Paperback)

Printed in the United States of America

DEDICATED TO

Kabi Samrata Birabara Upendra Bhanja (1670 - 1740)

Kabi Samrata, the Emperor of Poetry, was a late seventeenth and early eighteenth century Odia poet - composer of classical Odissi Music. He is most famous for his Odissi songs and Kabyas written in the Odia language, the sixth classical language of India. He was born at Kulada, a princely state in Bhanjanagar of Ganjam District in 1670 (opinions vary) and breathed his last at the age of seventy in 1740 (opinions vary). His period of poetry, *Riti juga* is also named after him as Bhanja juga. His notable works are Baidehisa Bilâsa, Lâbanyabati, Koti Brahmananda Sundari, Premasudhânidhi etc. which are classic poetry in Odia literature. He may be comparable with Kali Das. He even wrote a dictionary 'Geetabhidhana' in Odia for helping poets.

Upendra Bhanja wrote some 52 books of which only 22 are available now. Due to the absence of printing press, many of the hand-copied books have been lost. In 'Baidehisha Bilâsa', each line has been started with 'Ba', in 'Subhadra Parinaya' each line has been started with 'Sa', in 'Kalâ Koutuka' initial for every line is 'Ka', in 'Damayanti Bilâsa' with 'Da', in 'Satishâ Bilâsa' with initial 'Sa' in each line and in 'Padmâbati Parinaya' with 'Pa' initial in each line. The first published work of this famous poet is 'Rasapanchaka'. He has contributed 32,300 words to Odia language and literature. He is an incomparable poet of Odia literature. His imaginary ornamental expression by way of literary techniques of the classical Indian literature dominates with magnetic, lovable and intellectual manner.

Arun Chandra Sahu

PREFACE

"Give me the strength lightly to bear
my joys and sorrows.
Give me the strength to make my
love fruitful in service.
Give me the strength never to
disown the poor or bend my
knees before insolent might.
Give me the strength to raise my
mind high above daily trifles.

– 'Gitanjali'-36, Rabindranath Tagore

The title of this collection of poems is after its first long poem, 'The Silent Flute' and it seems not to be irrelevant to throw some light on this poem which depicts lucidly the divine love between god Krishna and goddess Râdhâ, their estrangement or separation, the reason behind breaking the flute by Krishna himself and their dermises. According to Hindu mythology SriKrishna was born from the womb of Debaki, wife of Basudeva, in the prison of King Kansha at Mathura of Uttar Pradesh at twelve midnight of eighth day of krushnapaksha i.e. from waxing moon (bright moon) towards waning moon (dark moon) in the month of Bhadraba (August-September) on Wednesday, the 19th July of 3228 B.C. Of course opinions vary regarding the birth date of Krishna, but it is unanimously confirmed that he was born on 8th day of Bhadraba krushnapaksha and this day is celebrated as 'Krushna Janmastami' through out India, even in foreign countries like America by the ISKON (International Society for Krishna Consciousness). It is a matter of concidence that Krishna is the eighth incarnation of god Vishnu, eighth child of mother Debaki, date of birth is also eighth of month Bhadraba, in his eighth year he loved Râdhâ who was also born on eighth day of suklapaksha of Bhadraba, of course before five years of birth of Krishna.

As Râdhâ was five years senior to Krishna, she might have born in 3233 B.C.. Her other names are Râdhikâ, Râdhârâni, Mâdhabi, Keshabi, Kishori. She is the Hindu goddess of compassion, devotion, tenderness and love and is the greatest among all Gopies, the supreme beloved and internal potency (hladini shakti) of Krishna. She resides in the heart of hearts and soul of Krishna and also in heaven, who is also believed as the incarnation of goddess Laxmi, the better half of Lord Vishnu. Some also consider her to be the woman figure of Krishna.

The pure, divine and intangible love of Râdhâ towards Krishna, climax at the soul level and mingling with the Brahma are all narrated vividly and exhaustively in many poems, epics and episodes. Râdhâ has also been characterized in vedic literature and Hindu epics. Also in Mahabharata, there is description of a woman named Radha, who happens to be the reared mother of Karna. Râdhâ is the prime goddess in Vaisnava religion. In the sixteenth century during Bhakti era, the divine love between Râdhâ and Krishna had been devoted at the supreme level. Radha is the main character in the famous poetry book, 'Gita Govind' by the twelfth century famous Odia poet Jayadeva. It is a dramatic lyrical unique poetry work in Indian literature and a source of inspiration to both medieval and contemporary Vaisnavism. It concentrates on Krishna's love with Radha and the gopis of Vrindavan. In it, Râdhâ is treated as the mistress not as the wife of Krishna. The divine love of Râdhâ-Krishna has also been narrated in 'Padma Purana', 'Brahma Vaibarta' and 'Devi Bhagabata Purana'.

Different opinions are there regarding the relationship of Râdhâ with Krishna. Some attribute their love as divine and nonphysical but some others are of opinion that their relationship is extramarital and physical. However, marriage between Râdhâ and Krishna was not solemnized. When Râdhâ asked Krishna: Why are you not marrying me ? Then Krishna replaced: Marriage is the union of two souls. But you and me have only one soul, indivisible. How shall I marry myself?

The Goudiyas consider the eternal spiritual love is the best exemplification of extramarital love among the two rashas (i.e. marital and extramarital) between Râdhâ and Krishna, where Radha and Krishna could communicate amongst themselves at the soul level even though they were separated. The other gopis had pure spiritual love with Krishna which was above physical level. Some opine that marriage between Râdhâ and Krishna was secretly solemnized in the forest of Brindavan which remained a secret among the general public. There are many stories about Râdhâ and Krishna, but it is unequivocally proclaimed that Râdhâ is the dazzling Hindu goddess of divine love, compassion and devotion.

There is a dual opinion regarding their death: whether Râdhâ died first or Krishna? But most people opine that in the last life, Radharani listening to the music of flute of Krishna, left her material body and united with the soul of Krishna and I have taken this as the prime theme of my first poem of this collection. Moreover after the desmise of Râdhâ, Krishna broke his flute by himself and threw into the forest. When Râdhârâni, his most beloved companion and queen of his heart, did not exist, to whom the music of flute of Krishna was the most lovable, made her mad of love, then why this flute will remain? There is not any special notes on: after how many years of Râdhâ's desmise, Krishna left his body? But it has been finalized that Krishna left his mortal body on 18th February 3102 B.C. when he was one hundred twenty five years seven months and six days old.

Some portrait the body colour of Krishna as deep black while some others depict as blue colour. Born in krushnapaksha, Krishna was black while Râdhâ was very fair born in suklapaksha. Krishna looks black for ordinary people, but with blue aura for real devotees, which is the aura of his eternal godly body, not of ordinary physical body. Blue colour is of the endless, unmeasurable eternal sky and space. The colour of the ocean or sea extending to the horizon is also blue. Moreover the aura that radiates from the god and goddess is of blue colour, just like Saraswati has another figure of Blue Saraswati. That which we can not imagine and out of our knowledge seems to be blue. The base of all elements of our universe believes to be blue. In Hindu mythology also Rama and Shiva have been depicted having blue coloured bodies but actually it is their blue aura which is emitted from their bodies. It has scientifically established that aura is a specific energy present around a body which is not expressed in the gross but present in the sukshma (subtle) body. He who is deeply engrossed in divine love can be fortunate to visualize this blue aura of Krisha or other gods. One person may be handsome but he cann't attract others without this aura. Only this blue aura can much deeply attract any person. For this reason, SriKrisha is the centre of attraction for all; and the attraction of any woman towards him seems to be natural. Moreover, the attraction of Râdhâ towards Krishna is very much extrme which is godly, spiritual and metaphysical.

According to some, the body of Krishna became blue after taking the poisonous milk of demoness Putanâ just like the throat of Shiva became blue after drinking the poison extracted from Samudra Manthana (churning of the ocean). But some others are of opinion that demoness Putana began to love boy Krishna by his mesmerism of blue aura. Any enemy can be hypnotized by the blue aura of Krishna and quits all his or her enmity. Further, the peacock's plumage (mayur chula) that he wears is centrally blue surrounded by green colouration.

On the other hand, body colour of Râdhâ is golden yellow which dazzles like the lightning. Râdhâ resides in the heart of Krishna like the existence of lightning in the deep black clouds in rainy days. Any narration, explanation or discussion made on Râdhâ and Krishna, still it seems to be incomplete. The love between Râdhâ and Krishna is at the supreme level in the world. Both are god and goddess of divine love.

Krishna is very fond of Râdhâ and his flute. His pleasant music of the flute is the bridge of their love. I have presented very negligibly about SriKrishna and Râdhâ in my poem. If any mistake is there, then I may be excused.

The second poem of this collection, 'The Second God' is meant for the plants who are depicted as second god and it is presented in the form of hymns in their praise. Animal kingdom is unthinkable without plants. Human beings and other animals are dependent upon the plants directly or indirectly mainly for food and oxygen. If no plant will exist in the earth, then the entire human civilization will be destroyed. Therefore, plants are the real second god. The third poem of this collection 'Desperation' is meant for SriKrishna and subsequent three poems also depict about Krishna. 'Madhava's World' is a caution to the modern youth of present mobile age which also contains some arrays of satire. Six poems on Corona have been presented which reflect some scientific thoughts. Apart from this, philosophy of life, contemporary social and the surrounding events, despair and desire, hopelessness and aloneness, emotion and aspiration, agony and sorrow, sadness and happiness of life and the melting time in the forthcoming death in the evening of life have been reflected in different poems. Many poems of its original Odia version have been published in various magazines and periodicals of Odisha and a few of its English translations have also been published in some magazines and souvenirs (coffee table magazines) for which the author is thankful to its editors.

I extend my heartfelt thanks to my better half, Vanumati, an eminent Odia writer, for her ungrudging support and inspiration during the preparation of the manuscript. My daughter Dr. Anoja, son Dr. Anubhav, son-in-law Dr. Saiprasad, daughter-in-law Er. Amruta and my relatives and friends are worthy to be thanked for their best wishes. I am also thankful to its publisher 'Black Eagle Books' of U.S.A. particularly to its Director Mr. Satya Pattnaik and India representative Mr. Ashok Parida for publishing this first international edition of the book elegantly and timely. Further, I thank 'Gudu DTP Art' of Cuttack for its nice typesetting. Ultimately I solicit divine blessings of god SriKrishna and goddess Râdhâ.

Arun Chandra Sahu

> 'I wandered, lonely as a cloud
> That floated on high o'er vales and hills,
> When all at once I saw a crowd,
> A host of golden daffodils;
> Beside the lake, beneath the trees,
> Fluttering and dancing in the breeze.
> – 'Daffodils', William Wordsworth.

Some Important Stanzas of this Poetry Collection

'Each and every moment she feels
as thousands of moments,
but days pass on one after another
in agony of separation in Gopapura.'
– The Silent Flute

'In the no moon night
the smiling stars have lost their smiles,
with one another they don't gossip
in the silent sky
filled with darkness, very deep.'
– The Silent Flute

'Flying her soul bird
mingled with the invisible soul
of Krishna for all time to come.'
– The Silent Flute

'Oh, our forefathers
of crores of years !
Without you, our bodies are empty
completely filled with vacuum.'
– The Second God

'Judgement of my case
is continuing years after years
in the court of law,
dried are my tears.'
      – Cage-bound

'Really my beauty
is my enemy,
my cuckoo's tone
is my foe,
my innocence
is my failure.'
      – A Bird of the Cage

'I'm a lonely shadow
of the pale afternoon
elongating gradually
to reach the horizon.'
      – A Lonely Shadow

'I feel as if someone is walking
like the shadow of darkness
behind me noiselessly
as one of my very close relatives.'
      – Noiselessly

'When he'll be entrapped
he'll recognize
the virtual world
that feels like the real world.'
      – Madhav's World

'Cross me smoothly
from the terrible clutch of
wounded, blooded, thorny, illusive
unconquerable, unmeasurable, inexpressible,
unfirable, indefatigable
ununderstandable time.'
                              – Wounded Sky

'In this horrible worldly affairs
my half body is non-illusive and real,
rest half is wounded, bruised and virtual.'
                              – Trishanku

'All the aspirations
may be fruitful or not,
all the desires
may be fulfilled or not,
but all the elements of mind
may be vanquished
to attain salvation.'
                              – Voidness

'Restlessly running
a frightened female deer,
scaredly looking
a pregnant tigress in fear.'
                              – Unperturbed God

'She is an idle bride,
when fully pregnant
delivers flood
overflowing both the banks.'
                              – Illumination

'Avoiding limitless desire and aspiration
search for the essence
beyond the senses.'
>   – Perfectness in Imperfectness

'Oh, Death God!
Take me in your lap
and again return me,
my lost childhood.'
>   – The Lost Childhood

'Already spent
all the episodes of life,
from son to father
father to grandfather
of both paternal and maternal.'
>   – Metamorphosis

'Lost would be my melodious sound
that wouldn't be uttered
from my mouth
in the invisible perch
of perpetual time.'
>   – In the Invisible Perch

'Through the smooth moss
adhering to the stone,
suddenly slipped my legs
down and down
in the quicksand of stream of time.'
>   – Swimming in the River

'All are games of time,
some are dazzling with damsels
some gloomy with darkness;
we all are wooden statues
in his invisible hands.'
– The Game of Time

'Bewildered we are.
In the quicksand of time
we all are metamorphosed
each into an invisible dot!
– In the Quicksand of Time

'As father was there
we felt the world
as a merry land.
Days were passing
like easy arithmetic.'
– As Father was there

'All are now memorable rainbows
in the sky of the past.
The camphor has been evaporated
leaving aside only
the white half shirt of my father.'
– My Father's Shirt

'But for a mere water bubble,
is there plenty of time
to visualize dream after dream of fondness
whose pre and post states
are full of voidness!'
– The Life

'Without battle
no one is agreeable
to give even a drop of water,
no one is ready to sacrifice
his own arrogance.'
— Battle

'The Ganges is now laughing
to her heart's content,
which many a project
couldn't perform for years together
can now be easily accomplished
by the miracle of a mere corona virus.'
— Thoughts of Corona -2

'After germination
if a seed becomes a tree
will it germinate again?'
— Down Memory Lane

CONTENTS

	Preface	07
1.	The Silent Flute	21
2.	The Second God	38
3.	Desperation	42
4.	Cage-bound	44
5.	A Bird of the Cage	46
6.	A Lonely Shadow	48
7.	Noiselessly	50
8.	Madhav's World	52
9.	World of Ownself	53
10.	Omnipresence	57
11.	Second Honeymoon	59
12.	Wounded Sky	61
13.	Trishanku	63
14.	Voidness	65
15.	Unperturbed God	67
16.	Illumination	69
17.	Perfectness in Imperfectness	71
18.	Water Mirror	73
19.	The Moon and the *Kâshatandi*	75
20.	The Lost Childhood	78
21.	Metamorphosis	80
22.	Acting	83

23.	In the Invisible Perch	85
24.	Swimming in the River	87
25.	The Blindman	89
26.	The Game of Time	92
27.	Inexpressible Time	94
28.	The Labyrinth of Illusion	96
29.	In the Quicksand of Time	98
30.	As Father was There	100
31.	My Father's Shirt	102
32.	In the Aspired Point	100
33.	The Life	106
34.	Tranquility	108
35.	The Battle	110
36.	The Soul	112
37.	Thoughts of Corona-1	114
38.	Thoughts of Corona-2	116
39.	Thoughts of Corona-3	118
40.	Thoughts of Corona-4	120
41.	A Poem on Corona	122
42.	Have come Alone, will go Alone	125
43.	White Screen	127
44.	Down Memory Lane	129
45.	Eternal Dazzling Star	131
46.	The Last Breath	133

The Silent Flute

|| One ||

How mesmerizing is the music of the flute !
How deep is the attraction
of a ten year old boy with bluish body
towards a thirteen year old fair girl ?
The girl has extreme attraction towards the boy.
Their attraction has altered
into deep attraction of love
which is metaphysical,
indescribable, divine and eternal.

Thrilled the entire Brundavan
with the unique music of the flute,
bewildered *Gopis* run automatically
to the bank of river *Yamunâ*
to meet the flute player
to amuse their ears, minds and hearts,
to take bath in the water of
metaphysical love.
Neighter anybody has yet played
such music on the flute

nor any one has listened to
such brilliant note on the flute
in this mortal world.

Leaving Brundavan
that boy in his youth worn the crown
of a different kingdom.
Around him circled queens,
queen consort, male and female servants,
but absent was the queen of his heart.
Crowd of the royal men in the
royal-court, but his mind was
towards that fair lady,
remembering her heartly
in the royal haven of the palace.
That fair lady also memorizing him deeply
as if became mad.

During sleep, dream and awakeness,
they could visualize each other
in the mirror of their souls
in the heart of their hearts
and in the invisible rendezvous.
Who will be like this
except Radha and Krishna
in this world ?

‖ Two ‖

Radha has been entangled with Krishna
Krishna also with Radha
for many ages.
Without Radha, Krishna is incomplete,
without Krishna, Radha is incomplete,
but with Radha, Krishna is complete.

> The soul is the medium
> for reciprocation of their love
> which is pure, true and eternal
> that they have adorned
> in their heart of hearts
> for their entire life span.

But alas!
A matter of great regret was that
Krishna could not marry Radha
who was his the most beloved gopi.
Their love was at stake
when Krishna left for Mathura
leaving Radhika alone in distress.

|| Three ||

Radha and the flute
are the most beloved for Krishna,
no other person or article.
The art of playing flute
is the clue of his love
in which are thrilled and enchanted
all the gopis, including Radha
the chief consort of Krishna.
Remains always with Krishna
his most dearest flute
like the shadow that does not
leave at all,
by the playing of which
the fire of love of Radha
moves up, towards the heaven,
spreads like wildfire.

    Wearing the peacock's blue plumage
    Krishna is a blue magnet,
    easily attracting Radha,
    Gopanganas, all mingle wholy
    in his divine soul;
    he happens to be their supreme lover.

|| Four ||

After Krishna left for Dwaraka
alone was Radha, very alone.
Innocent time of her
couldn't pass without Krishna
in Gopapura.
Going to river Yamuna
to take bath, sitting and sitting
on its bank for hours together,
she sketches on its sand strange images,
staring constantly at the
waves of love that gradually
enlarge and mingle in the
bank of the river.

> In the next moment
> she listens to the
> tune of the flute of Krishna
> in the murmuring sound of Yamuna.
> While returning with water filled earthen pot
> becomes alarmed as if some one
> has pressed her two lotus eyes
> by two hands from backside.

Isn't it the naughtiness of Krishna ?
Reaching home she sees
the curd filled earthen pot empty.
Are the curds flown away
by the flute tune of Krishna
or in the current of Yamuna water ?

Each and every moment she feels
as thousands of moments,
but days pass on one after another
in agony of separation
in Gopapura.
Night after night extinguishes
with repeated long inhale and exhale.
The flute of Krishna visualizes Radha
in the full moon,
listens to his sweetened flute-tune
in the moon-lit night again and again,
drinks to her heart's content
that stream of elixir.
Asks in the no moon day
to the question mark of *Saptarshi**:
Have you seen my Kanha anywhere !
How is he ?
Is he remembering me ?

While visualizing the deep dark
clouds in the sky,
Radha could see Krishna being extremely thrilled
in mind and heart but in the next moment

was losing her sense
time and again.
What a deep love,
no one can imagine !

* *Saptarshi* : The asterism of the Big Dipper (part of the constellation of Ursa Major) with seven stars representing seven rishis namely: *Kratu, Pulaha, Pulastya, Atri, Angira, Vashistha* and *Marichi* and it looks like a question mark.

|| Five ||

Peeps the time with bouquet of dreams,
questions Radha: Will you go to Dwaraka
disposing all your worries ?
Who will now be attracted
towards dry dull lusterless Brindavan ?
Rushed Radha to Dwaraka emotionally
but reaching there she hears
about the marriage of Krishna
with *Rukuni* and *Satyabhâmâ*.
However she is not purturbed or annoyed.
She is a mendicant of pure love,
the climax of a mountain of love
to whom can't touch
criticism, condemnation and junk of love.

> Krishna becomes thrilled
> at the sight of Radha,
> spends days and nights
> with gossip crowned with divine love.
> Who has recognized Radha in Dwaraka ?
> She is an unknown lady there.
> Requests Radha : Keep me in this
> royal palace as a *Devika**.

* *Devika* : little goddess

|| Six ||

To spend one day in that palace
Radha feels as if many days have elapsed.
Waiting for the opportunity
to visualize Kanha
she never hesitates to fully utilize it,
again becomes a mendicant of love
by spending intimate time
gossiping with Kanha.

> However she feels ardently
> as if an invisible eclipse
> has covered their divine love.
> Kanha is now not like the
> previous Krishna.
> Where has gone the mesmerizing,
> amazing, spiritual music of flute of Krishna
> sitting on the branch of a Kadamba tree
> near the bank of Yamuna?
> Where has gone his divine blue aura
> that has been emitted from his
> eternal godly body?

Radha only visualizes
that divine aura and figure of Krishna
in her divine eyes,
but he looks deep dark for others.
Where have they the concentration of devotion
to behold such divine physique ?
It is eternal, immeasurable,
endless and infinite,
like the cloudless sky of summer
looks blue to our physical eyes.

|| Seven ||

After tide comes the ebb
in the heart of Radha.
Firmly decides she
not to stay in the palace,
will go away to long distances
and establish a deep spiritual relation
with Krishna in her later life.

    Couldn't know Radha
    where is she going,
    as if she becomes insane.
    In last part of her life
    alone she was, very much alone.
    Gradually melt her lonely moments,
    only her friends are the silent banks of Yamuna,
    its water of tears,
    and the pale branches of Kadamba.
    Day by day her mortal body
    becomes unenergetic and incompetent.

It seems the sky is vanishing eventually;
its blue colour becomes pale and dull.

The moon of the full moon night
appears to be alone, very much alone,
clinging to her eyes are tear drops,
the cool moon-light becomes warmer
like the warm air of mild summer.
In the no moon night
the smiling stars have lost their smiles.
With one another they don't gossip
in the silent sky
filled with darkness, very deep.

> The distant hills cry sobbingly
> in the lonely mid-day;
> all of a sudden with loud peculiar sound
> the birds fall down
> with their faces down.
> All the memories vanish
> in the invisible darkness.
> All the carefully stored dreams
> break into pieces
> in Kanha's absence.

The cracking sound of bones
is heard, the blood of the pale flesh
is drying day by day.
The fair skin covering them
becomes darkened and crumpled
drawing the artwork of Krishna.
Once very much beautiful
all become pale and dull
in the curse course of time,

now not in need of Radha.
Tearing them she offers to Krishna.
Past, present and future of Radha are
as if tagged with Krishna
from time immemorial
which He knows best.

>Aspiration of Radha :
>One day surely will come Krishna,
>her life of life, treasure of life.
>She waits:
>When will
>her desire be fulfilled ?

‖ **Eight** ‖

All of a sudden appeared Krishna,
the flute lover, before Radha.
Asking Radha something from her,
but Radha communicated her dissent
through her silence.
Again Krishna requested,
at last Radha wished looking at him-
let Krishna play his flute
for the last time.

    Krishna took his dear flute,
    played extremely well
    with the rhythm of divine tune
    which thrilled the entire world,
    astonished all the birds and animals,
    humans and demons.
    For days and nights
    he played on the flute
    the music of which was filled with
    vibration of a different
    tune of pathos.

In that tune of the flute
was thrilled Radharani;
listening continuously to the divine music of the flute
she abandoned her mortal body
of *Panchamahâbhuta**.

Flying her soul bird
mingled with the invisible soul
of Krishna for all time to come.
The final episode of divine love
will dazzle eternally
in the canvas of endless time.

*Panchamahâbhuta : It stands for five physical elements : earth (Khit), water (App), fire (Tej), air (Maruta) and space or sky (Byoma). These elements have a great significane in the nature and human life as well.

|| Nine ||

Couldn't tolerate Krishna
the demise of Radha, his queen of hearts.
If his most beloved Radha couldn't remain
why should remain his flute?
Breaking the flute into pieces
he threw into the bushes
of the forest.
In lament, the dear flute of Krishna
by breakage of his association
with his lord uttered :
What is my fault, Lord?
Why are you quiting me?
Can I live without you?
Just like Krishna cann't remain
without Radha, the flute
cann't remain without Krishna.
I'm emersing my life today
by the side of the bush.

> Overwhelmed with joy said the bush :
> Oh Lord, my life is now filled with bliss
> by gaining the association of the pieces of the flute
> that you liked very much
> and kept in close association of yours.

Vowed SriKrishna :
He would never play any flute
or any other musical instrument
till his demise.
After thirty six years
of the battle of Mahabharata
Krishna was injured
by the arrow of *Jârâ Sabara*
who thought the leg of sleeping Krishna
as the ear of a deer.
Of course, Krishna had pardoned him,
ultimately left his mortal body
from the mortal world
spending one hundred twenty five years.

Vamished from this earth
the last symbol of an eternal divine love.
No body will listen to, in this world,
such rare magnetic music of the flute.
Where is now Radharani to appeal :
Oh Krishna !
Play again thy flute
that had given to the past,
closing my eyes I'll listen to that sweet tune
and again I'll be a lunatic of love.

The Second God

Oh, plants !
You're the energy,
you're the orderliness,
you're the food and life,
you're the oxygen,
you're our master, saviour, creator
and what not !

>You're our rise and set
>up and down, life and death
>hell and heaven
>elixir of immortality
>and poisonous red fruit with blackness
>inside (*Mahâkâla phala*)
>indestructible, innumerable and numerable,
>smooth and hard, soft like cotton threads,
>strong like the thunder
>and floating like the clouds,
>austere like the mountains,
>highest peak like the Himalayas.

Oh, plants!
Glowing you're inside the deep ocean,
cool in the high temperature of the desert,
flame of fire in the biting cold
of the north and south pole.
In the flooded-water, living banyan leaf
on which is present the invisible creator
of this world, of this universe.
Our millions of bows down before you,
millions of salutes to you.

> Oh, our forefathers
> of crores of years!
> without you, our bodies are empty
> completely filled with vacuum.
> Oh, our donor of life,
> donor of genes
> indirectly donor of blood,
> root cause of all our characters,
> praising you as much as we can,
> still will be negligible.

You're are our rice and food,
shelter and clothes,
all extraordinary sculptures,
Darubramha, pretty paintings
and attractive artworks,
all such thoughts and notions.
You're the colours of our lives :
violet, indigo, blue, green, orange
yellow and red,

white you are, admixture of all colours
and black in their absence,
storehouse of all leaves, flowers
and fruits you are.

> You're the peace, calmness and love,
> companion and bosom friend.
> You're the god of all gods,
> friend and foe are all yours,
> without envy, jealousy and hatred,
> soul and divinity of the nature queen
> adorned with all virtues,
> dazzling, glowing your each molecule and atom,
> embellishing your elements.
> Without your presence
> the world will be horrified,
> the earth will crack, the sky will be fired
> dreadful icebergs will flow
> from both the poles,
> entire earth will be paralysed,
> will float in the water
> of universal dissolution
> as a round, helpless, strange queer dead body.

Of course again there will be a new creation
after the universal dissolution.
Time will take birth
in the cradle place of *Mahâsunya*
as an extremely minute element
from which you'll reappear again
and thereafter we shall.

Oh, our dear plants !
We're inviting you whole heartedly.
Let you exist eternally.
You're the only factor
to profect our existence.
You're really
our second god,
again millions and millions of salutes to you,
oh, our dear plants !

Desperation

A blunder I made,
for worshipping couldn't offer blue lilies
on the lotus feet of blue Krishna,
that blossomed in my muddy pond
for many years.
My heart was broken and broken.

    Birth after birth elapsed
    memorizing His words.
    Lest I may forget
    his blue radiating face
    which looks like deep dark cloud
    for others,
    I kept open my eyes
    days and nights
    imagining his face with peacock's plumage.

Where have I that divine eyes
to visualize his astonishing
appearance of universe ?
After engulfing soil of delusion
is he showing his trembling mouth
to angry Yashodâ, his foster mother ?

Now in my pale pond
blue lilies are not blossoming.
Couldn't imagine
how to offer him blue lilies.
In the meantime
yugas after yugas have elapsed.
The blue lily had a state of desperation
as all the time had elapsed.
Alas ! even a single moment did not remain
for the innocent blue lily.

Cage-bound

|| One ||

I'm a cage-bound furious animal,
lion or tiger.

> Furiosity is my ornament,
> golden crown;
> without it I've no existence,
> very dull and energyless.
> My falseless wild roaring
> trembles miles and miles away.
> To visualize my angry acting
> congregate thousands of people;
> nature-lovers come from distant places
> to observe my dreadful natural image.

|| Two ||

I'm a cage-bound human,
iron chains are in my hands and legs.
People say I'm a dangerous criminal.
Judgement of my case
is continuing years after years
in the court of law,
dried are my tears!

> I don't care
> the delayed judgement,
> what had I done is correct.
> If I've killed
> the injustice, oppression, suppression,
> infidelity, unruly, corruption of the society
> am I the culprit?

Oh, Krishna!
You're the only saviour,
consider my case
in your esteemed court.

A Bird of the Cage

In this limited space of iron cage
completely shattered is my independence.

      My dreams are the multicoloured clouds
      of the blue sky,
      layers of greenness of the trees and creepers.
      Natural love of the leaves,
      flowers and fruits
      are scarce and unavailable here.
      Even if I'm fed with
      foreign fruits, milk and mineral water
      am I satisfied ?

Really my beauty
is my enemy,
my cuckoo's tone
is my foe,
my innocence
is my failure.

      I'm again requesting
      in my pressured chirping:

Oh, SriKrishna, Muralimohan,
the wonderful fluter of the world !
Please come once to me
to relieve my miserable time.
You're the incarnator
who saved the life of a bird and
her kids by covering them with a big bell
of an elephant
in the war field of *Kurukshetra*.
Is anything unknown to you ?
Oh, my lord SriKrishna !

•

A Lonely Shadow

I'm a lonely shadow
of the pale afternoon
elongating gradually
to reach the horizon.

>But am I running
>without thinking anything,
>without caring the ups and downs
>of the crumpled road
>to touch the divine feet of *Râdhâ*
>to listen to the tune
>of the flute of SriKrishna,
>to visualize his dazzling blue rays.
>But alas !
>where have I the fortune of having
>such deep devotion
>to obtain the divine sight ?

Facing a lot of misfortune,
drinking the tears and blood
on the path of thorns,
digesting the grief and pathos of life,

swallowing easily the mixture
of laugh and cry,
jumping from land to the sky
now I'm hanging in the
prop roots of banyan
which is whirling so much that
sometime I may be detached
and fall in an invisible, undesirable
untradeable and narrow tunnel.

    Nobody will know it
    in this earthy stage of illusion
    except one.

Noiselessly

Noiselessly I can easily
converse with you lonely.

    What is the need of
    making such noise pollution
    in this deeply polluted environment?
    All the plants of the entire earth
    are threatened, endangered,
    pressurized by unseen dreadful apprehension.
    It is not sure
    when will be there
    an explosion in a noiseless moment ?

Noiselessly I'm walking singly
in this crowded market of the world.
From distant places is heard
the sobbingly weeping of a doe.
I'm feeling
as if a stone is falling
when a stick falls.
No dear ones are there beside me
to pour a sip of water in my mouth !

In my both sides
are standing noiselessly
skyscrapers of concrete jungle.
Somebody is making me swim
in the sea of winds.
My darkness is weeping
in the light of lightning;
the voice of my throat
is breaking gradually
in the dreadful sound of the thunder.
In the very heavy rain
my hairroots are full to the brim,
appearing there red and blue lilies.
When will they take bath of sound
without any noise?
But I'm feeling as if
all are invisible, imperceptible.

Still my path,
I feel, is not ending.
All of a sudden, I feel
as if someone is walking
like the shadow of darkness
behind me noiselessly
as one of my very close relatives !

Madhav's World

How much does Madhav know
about this world !
It seems, his childhood
has not yet been completed.
Still sitting on the sofa,
holding a smart phone,
he pretends not to have eaten.
In doubt when his mother asks,
he replies that he has eaten dark chocolate
but has eaten actually
some prohibited items hiddenly.

    Is there any courage
    of today's mother to ask:
    Open your mouth
    I'll see
    what have you really eaten ?
    Like mother *Yashodâ* was asking:
    Open your mouth *Krishna*
    have you eaten soil ?
    Opened the mouth Krishna
    and seeing the entire universe
    inside his mouth
    Yashodâ was astonished and fainted.

But will today's mothers be fainted?
Rather they will laugh like that of Mona Lisa,
and will tell: My son is very clever and naughty,
knows the art of converting
the lie to truth.
Like the smell of young leaves
of sacred basil seedling,
I smell that one day he will be a minister,
will show me the entire world
in luxurious chartered aeroplane.

> How has recognized Madhav
> love and betrayal ?
> Youth is temporal
> like the shedding of *Gangasiuli*,
> the queen of the night.
> Better to reap from the
> college corridor and the garden
> the very dear pathos
> which is eternal like the polestar,
> will always stand before you
> like your obedient shadow.
> But Madhav is in need of
> *Krushnachudâ*, the peacock flower
> having youth forever.

How has known Madhav
his boy or girl friends ?
Especially his girlfriends,
with whom he chats in smart phones
and takes them to the hotels and restaurants
to feed them with dum biriyani
and tandoori chicken.

Of course, foreign champagne
he has not yet tested.

> Very proud are his parents.
> Anyhow seven girlfriends our son has
> for seven days.
> *Krishna* had thousands of *Gopis*,
> but only seven girlfriends our Madhav has,
> so what is wrong with him?
> Will the world be in a state of topsy-turvy
> or will the holy books be immoral ?
> In today's world
> if there is no girlfriend
> will he be counted as a smart boy ?
> Out of seven days, the girl
> who goes on Sunday, is the smartest
> of all having different postures;
> as if the world of Madhav
> she has acquired.
> She is his queen honeybee !

How much does Madhav recognize them ?
It seems, he hasn't yet
fully know them.
Only holding a smartphone
he pretends to know everything.
When he'll be entrapped
he'll recognize the virtual world
that feels like the real world.

●

World of ownself

Cool breeze of independence
is blowing in your own world.
Any corner of the time you look
you can go there easily, fearlessly,
smoothly and without hesitation.

> In your own world
> the sun will rise and set
> according to your own will.
> If you wish
> moon will peep during daytime
> in your roof of the world;
> will laugh merrily and
> spread over you bed-spread of
> delicate, cool and white moonlight.
> In that bed-spread
> flowers of twinkling stars will
> be beautifully designed.
> If you wish
> you may be mesmerized or not
> that depends upon your will.

In your own world are
layers of green sarees,
beautiful decoration of carpets,
of multi-coloured flowers.
Dry, rude, dilapidated, hot
latitude and longitude of summer
are not there.
Hilstone, snowfall, thunder
and lightning, bone-biting cold
of winter are also scarce.

> Your own world is filled with
> rhythmic music of rain,
> murmuring sound of stream and river,
> buzzing sound of bumblebee,
> budging of the red lotus,
> flying here and there
> the disobedient butterflies,
> continuous singing of the cuckoos
> sitting on the branches of mango tree,
> silvery laugh of your
> never ending youth,
> no birth of agony, despair
> and suffering in your kingdom.

All are possible only
if you utter 'Khul ja sim sim'.

Omnipresence

He is climbing carefully
the snaky ladder of time.
But when he is climbing
one hundred smooth steps,
next moment he is falling down
many a thorny and rocky steps
where fine art
of his bloody foots appear.
Who is his friend
and who is his foe ?

    Still never is dried or gloomy
    his river of aspirations,
    never exhibits false pride.
    Day by day it sweels jovially
    touching both the brims,
    marches ahead in curvy paths.
    In his heart as if there are
    moonlight of hundred moons,
    and energy of thousand suns !

He'll never step down
from his own dignified throne

lest there may be holocaust of the earth.
In front is seen the sea,
casuarina trees are seen faintly,
roaring sound of the boasting sea
is heard.
Over the sand are artworks of the beach,
his prime destination
to spend much of his time,
to fill the high waves
with the colour of the blood
to wash hills of his carefully kept
grief, jealousy, despair and envy.

>But he has vowed,
>by breaking the proud waves of the sea
>one after another
>will reach near Him
>treading the ladder of the
>distant horizon,
>whose existence he has
>not yet imagined,
>not felt as impossible,
>although at a very fine level
>one day he has cherished
>His omnipresence

●

Second Honeymoon

In the golden jubilee
of our marriage anniversary
we are planning to fly to Switzerland
in our sweet second honeymoon.

> From last month
> Mahesh babu has gone
> to Bali island
> in the silver jubilee
> of their marriage anniversary.
> Sitting on the blue sea shore
> catching fish by *bansi*,
> he has sent the photographs
> in WhatsApp.

Has gone to Japan
Dinesh babu with his better half
to attend a conference.
Listening to Sayonara songs in the evening
while visualizing water dance
sitting in the park.

Subash babu, a very nice gentleman,
in LTC has gone to Andaman
along with his lovely wife
to visualize the black water,
the cellular jail where the Indian prisoners
were tortured very badly
by the English.
Swimming along with the coloured fishes
in the deep blue water of the sea,
gossiping with the shark
in primeval language,
painting his body
with the colour of the butterflies,
in the romantic moonlight
he is murmuring in the ear of his wife:
Oh, my dear, my love for you
is as bright as the moon;
such a magnificent moonlit night
in my life time I've never seen.

But in the golden jubilee
of our wedding anniversary
are we really have a trip
to Switzerland
or to Daringbadi,
the Kashmir of Odisha ?

●

Wounded Sky

I'm a wounded sky,
blood is oozing out silently
painting me red,
but no body is there to pacify.

    Impatient I'm
    by the streams of blood,
    covering my invisible body,
    filled with unbearable pain
    in all my nerves and nerve-lets.
    The entire earth is covered with
    dark clouds of despair.

In that I seek
His honest blessings,
while in the jungle where
light doesn't penetrate,
putting my steps irregularly
in the thorny snaky path,
discovering a piece of glittering diamond
in the deep dark tunnel of coal,
visualizing a dazzling pearl

while searching the oysters
in the dreadful deep sea.

    I recite noiselessly a hymn
    closing my both hands,
    offer my prayer lying fully on the land:
    Cross me smoothly
    from the terrible clutch of wounded, blooded,
    thorny, illusive, unconquerable,
    unmeasurable, inexpressible, unfirable,
    indefatigable, unundersta ndable time.

•

Trishanku

In half darkness and half light
in half communication and half non-communication
in half completeness and half incompleteness
I feel my life like half half,
half body and half soul
as if my physical or metaphysical body
has been half-built.

    In this horrible worldly affairs
    my half body is non-illusive and real
    rest half is wounded, bruised and virtual.
    In the red roses of my half garden
    the dew drops are glittering, dazzling
    like the chain of pearls of aspiration,
    in the half tender rays
    of the half sun
    in the half morning.

In the front half-shown path
are elegantly standing half-cut mirages.
Half-stars are falling
from the half sky

on that path.
I'm picking them,
setting them after cleaning
in the half shelves
of the half-built shisham-wooden almirah.

> My dreams half-opened and half-claded
> by the half saree of my better half,
> are as if made into halves.
> In the half moonlight
> of the eighth day moon
> they are flying from the
> lower half land to the upper eternal sky
> but hanging like *Trishanku**
> as if for all time to come.

A murmuring sound I heard
from a foreign land:
Oh, I'm also
in the same state,
hung between the real
and the virtual.

●

Trishanku: *Trishanku* is a famous character in Hindu mythology who is hanged upside down between heaven and earth, belonging nowhere.

Voidness

All the aspirations
may be fruitful or not,
all the desires
may be fulfilled or not,
but all the elements of mind
may be vanquished
to attain salvation.

> All the limbs of delusion and stinginess
> be silent, numbed, lustreless
> and in deep meditation.
> Indulging in the internal nothingness
> of the world,
> roaming easily in the
> external emptiness of time
> throw eventually all the
> six enemies of mind:
> Kâma (desire), Krodha (anger),
> Lobha (greed), Moha (delusion),
> Mada (arrogance) and Mâtsarya (jealousy)
> into the voidness.
> Convert all happiness and unhappiness

>   laugh and cry, enviousness and
>   hostility, fame and disgrace
>   into one entity, undivided,
>   being engrossed in detachment.

As if all become void
in the emptiness, great emptiness.
He can visualize to his heart's content
the existence of world of *Nirguna**
which in our worldly bodies,
the divine power of understanding
is zero, completely zero.

●

---

*Nirguna: an important term in the philosophy of Vedanta, which shares its roots with yoga, because it's often used to raise the question of whether *Brahman* is with or without qualities (distinction).

Unperturbed God

Silence has prevailed
throughout the night.
Being wounded and blooded
the poor girl has been released
from the mouth of a tiger,
and lying shattered in the corner of a house
like a motionless mute stone.

>As if the entire earth
>has been stunned, dumbfounded.
>Tons of tears have been
>compressed in the eyes
>but not oozing out a single drop of tear.

However, getting extremely angry
the lightning is firing the sky,
the severe thunderclap is stunning the ears,
roaring the black running clouds
are raining cats and dogs.
The earth is shattered by thunderstorms.
Restlessly running
a frightened female deer

scaredly looking
a pregnant tigress in fear.

    In some remote corners
    of the earth,
    such a girl child, a young lady,
    a woman or an old woman
    might have been lying
    shattered touching her face
    hardly on the floor
    being perturbed by unspeakable,
    unbearable agony
    but deep silence might have been
    prevailing throughout the empire,
    as if nothing happened !

Is God now-a-days callous, unperturbed?
Not a single word
is coming out of his mouth!
Is his intension
to end the Kaliyug soon!

        •

Illumination

How arrogant is the river
flowing zigzag
waving her thin waist in summer !
She is an idle bride,
when fully pregnant
delivers flood
overflowing both the banks.

    Cann't you create a flood
    touching the horizon
    and the sky?
    Crossing the boundary
    of the golden triangle,
    jumping from Kanyakumari
    to Kashmir,
    from the sand dunes
    of the Thar desert
    touching the skyscraper proud trees
    of Cherrapunji,
    drenching the milky white
    disdainful wings of
    miraculous geese

roaming elegantly
in the colourful splendour
of Manasarovar !

In this territory
is heard war bigul,
but in the other territory
greedy eyes are becoming ready
with agglomerate sarcastic glancing.
Waiting for the opportunity
to extremely vibrate
the silent sky
with gun firing, grenades and bombing
and to brighten the illumination
smeared with blood.

●

Perfectness in Imperfectness

You're a red rose,
sharp sword
that tears the heart lustfully.
Tears of love are sprinkled around.
You make void in perfectness,
but fill perfectness
in baskets of imperfectness.
Avoiding limitless desire and aspiration
search for the essence
beyond the senses.

> Drowning in that essence
> as if not drowning,
> stay invisible
> on the mast of a directionless ship.
> In the restless waves of restless sea
> the oceanic storm roars fiercely;
> treading the land and horizon
> bugles to dance violently
> o'er the entire earth's chest.

Your sharp weapon
abruptly calms
the sea, sky, horizon
and the mast of the ship
where your symbol glitters,
smells heart-touchingly,
dazzles like the memorial of
undescribable contentment
till the existence of the question-mark symbol
of the Saptarshi constellation.

Water Mirror

Taking birth sparkled
in the worldly existence,
when visible appeared
in the invisible stage.

> Beeped every moment
> in the unglowing fire,
> thrilled with excitement
> in the youth of agony and aspiration.
> While treading the spiny path
> pasted the blood-shed of the foots
> o'er the forehead like sandalwood.

Made a garland of tears
of divine blessings
and untold contentment
around the neck.
Became overwhelmed
with the worldly mortal affairs
like blue-necked *Shiva*.

The weeping of the female dove
was resounding time and again
in the deep dark sky.
Was no body hearing that ?
Standing aside
beyond the vision of the people,
couldn't anyone aim
at the eyes of the scoundrel
for shooting arrow of punishment
gazing down the mirror of
crystal clear water ?

The Moon and the *Kâshatandi*

Stepping down from the
clear sky of the full moon night,
laughing merrily the moon asked
to the *Kâshatandi** swinging in
slow blowing wind like the white waves of the sea:
How are you *Kâshatandi* ?
Why is your face devoid of jubilation !

    Let us play hide and seek
    with the congregate white clouds.
    Hiding myself I'll search you
    among the river banks, casuarina jungle,
    and long line of paddy fields.
    You'll search me
    looking here and there,
    if will touch me
    under the bedcover of
    moon-light spreading over the
    entire land and horizon,
    laugh will bloom
    in your face.

Mixing my laugh with
your laugh will resound
in the chest of the
unperturbed mountain.
However, in the bright sky
the stars are pale, feeble, muted
present randomly with dried faces
but layers of moon shine
are spread over their faces.

On the other,
behold the arrogance of the stars
in the darkness of the sky
of new moon night,
proudly twinkling their eyes
throughout the sky.
However, the face of *Kâshatandi*
is looking bright in the deep dark.
Darkness is ruling disdainfully
in the absence of moonlight.
In a palace
on the other side of the earth,
the moon has taken rest
with her companion, the moon shine
for twenty-four hours
as she is tired of
running so many days
in the sky field
without taking any break.

After rest
the moon will show her face
looking like your curved eye brow.

●

Kâshatandi : Kans grass *Saccharum spontaneum* (scientific name), a perennial grass native to Indian subcontinent which flowers in autumn. These flowers create the delusion of a thick white blanket near river banks.

The Lost Childhood

How helpless is man's life
at the beginning and at the end !
Ultimately mingles in fire and smoke
in the sky, in void and the great void,
the *mahasunya*.

> How helpless
> in the stretcher of agony,
> on the white bed
> of the hospital!
> How helpless are the eyeballs !
> Two hands
> unable to move,
> the energy has been diminished.
> Although the mouth is opened
> unable to utter any word;
> the larynx is completely functionless.

Someone staying above the sky in void
judging the deeds
prescribes how many days

he or she will crawl
on the thorny carpet of time.

>Now there is no dream
>to dream.
>The sense of visualization
>is not willing to watch the television.
>The hand is not moving
>to compose poems;
>no treasure of thoughts
>to think.
>Dried are the taste buds of the tongue
>to taste variety of foods.
>The eardrums are unable to hear
>romantic or melodious Hindi songs.

Oh, Death God !
Take me in your lap
and again return me
my lost childhood !

Metamorphosis

Initially my father
joined government service at Aska,
then at Bhubaneswar
as inspector of schools,
was staying in unit one
in a type four quarters.
During nineteen fifties
Bhubaneswar was in its childhood
playing in the open field,
eating *kantei koli*[1], *fârshâ koli*[2]
roaming in the bushy jungle.

    Once my father visited
    a school near Khandagiri,
    took me in his Philips bicycle.
    While returning it rained
    cats and dogs, completely drenched
    in water, in lightning thunderstorm
    uttering 'Ram Ram' in thrilled tone
    we returned.
    Next day I suffered from cough and cold
    and severe fever.

Mother was furious:
Why have you taken my small child
for a long distance?
But I wasn't fearful
as my father was with me.

Once my younger brother was lost.
While searching we found him
standing near a saw mill
and looking how the wooden logs
were sawed !
Now we feel
as if our aspirations are being sawed
into pieces by the invisible saw.

We were eating groundnuts
in the cone like paper packets,
running to catch butterflies,
counting the number of
bicycles or rarely any scooter
passing our front road.
At night we were visualizing
the rows of ants
under electric lamp.
Once I suffered from severe typhoid fever
when I was reading in class one.

Pleasant wind was blowing
during summer evening,
Krushnachudâ flowers were laughing merrily.
Varied coloured clouds
were playing hide and seek in the sky.

Our football was reaching the blue sky.
The heart of the time
was charmed and thrilled
with the taste of varieties of mangoes.

But now in the evening of life
we are not allowed to taste
the sweet mangoes,
as blood sugar is enhancing.
As if to dream sweet dreams
is denied, the life is
full of bitter taste
like the bitter gourds.
Gradually deterioration is
peeping its face;
the earthen lamp is
going to extinguish.

Already spent
all the episodes of life:
from son to father,
father to grandfather
of both paternal and maternal.

●

[1] *Kantei koli* : a small tasty berry of deep reddish black colour known as wild jujujbe in English, *Ziziphus oenoplia* (scientific name), Jungal Kul Makai in Hindi, Pariki in Telgu and Kantei Koli in Odia.

[2] *Fârshâ koli* (in Odia): a small tasty berry of reddish brown colour when mature and tastes sweet and sour.

Acting

Why are you quarrelling
with me always
in small matters
in this Kaliyuga,
full of conflict and sin !

    Even if I'm playing
    some tricks not to quarrel,
    still are you touching my heart
    or acting not to touch my heart
    in this invisible stage
    of the world !

In this daily quarrel,
day after day
I'm feeling an internal void
or feeling as if
you are loving me more
when you are quarrelling
with me more,
otherwise, can a man quarrel
with an unknown man without hesitation

in an ordinary matter
that seems to be extraordinary !

    Now I think
    when you act to quarrel with me
    in my simple untoward incident,
    I'll unfold my soundless laughs
    with ecstasy and stretch my
    obedient hands towards you
    for which purpose
    that though you've understood
    but would pretend
    not to be aware of.
    Still, I'll not return back,
    rather will proceed forward
    in my destination
    without hesitation.

●

In the Invisible Perch

Why are you poking your nose
in my every statement
for which I'm not worried !

    When you feel headache,
    the same also I feel.
    Even if we try hundred times
    not to feel it,
    still we feel headache
    not in the natural place
    but in some invisible,
    unthinkable, pin-pointed place
    with seclusion.
    With a long seigh
    my entire longevity mingles
    in your lone longevity of
    bloodless, fleshless body.

By floating I'll go away
in the snaky river of
your chuckle laughter,

in amazing moonlight in somnolence,
in the enhanced thrilling
of dazzling stars those look dull and pale.
Lost would be my melodious sound
that wouldn't be uttered from my mouth
in the invisible perch
of perpetual time.

●

Swimming in the River

I was diving into the lukewarm water
of the river
clasping your hands tightly.

>Through the smooth moss
adhering to the stone,
suddenly slipped my legs
down and down
in the quicksand of stream of time.
Before whirling felt I
as if you pulled my hand
up and up by your
invisible witchcraft.
I was in topsy-turvy
over the water surface.
Though I wasn't acting
not to know the art of swimming,
at once I could learn
the art of all sorts of swimming
by your invisible magic.

Then like an expert swimmer
I could swim in various patterns of swimming
crushing the upper, middle and lower layers
of river water.

While swimming inside the water
coloured fishes were also swimming
in various postures,
caressing my body
talking with me easily
by the language of dancing
of their eyeballs.

    Holding your hand warmly
    I told: Come my dear,
    as I have learnt
    the art of swimming,
    I'll instruct you
    how to swim freely
    in the very deep water,
    how to dive into the
    abysmal depths of river water.

Afterwards thought I:
Who am I ?
Everything is your invisible wizardry.
What shall I instruct you for swimming ?
In my hidden sky is peeping
an unforeseen, unpredictable fear.
All you know my dear,
only pretending as if
you know nothing
that I sense from your
cute blue eyes !

●

The Blindman

I've eyes,
beautiful eyebrows which I can raise
clear eyeballs
which can also rotate,
can give you a look of annoyance
or disdain.

> I can close my eyes
> if I wish to close
> and also at night.
> Can open my eyes
> if I wish
> but alas, unable to see anything !
> All say that
> I'm a blindman.
> Only I hear that
> there is light and also darkness,
> how lovely are the rose flowers,
> how beautiful are the sunrise
> and sunset !

Just I try to feel it
in my mind,
but unable to imagine.
Oh my God !

My heart is filled with
love, affection and emotion.
Blood of desire and aspiration
is flowing perfectly,
but I feel something is absent
which I don't care.

Although I'm blind in sight
but not in my deeds,
not even in the networking of my mind.
I can dream at night
where charming angles
come down from the sky
to visualize the blue sea
of my eye and to pat
its innumerable foamy blue waves.

Although I'm blind
but trying day and night
to reach the top of my goal.
However, in this world
some are blind for wealth,
some for name and fame,
some for the post of political leadership,
some for the lease of coal mines

and even some are blind for charming
and beautiful heroines !

> In history, there were also
> blind persons who were
> though blind physically
> still blind for the sake their sons,
> even though streams of blood may flow
> in the Kurukshetra
> for eighteen days.

●

The Game of Time

When you reach the ripe old age
there wouldn't be drops of tear
or blood to ooze out
from your body.

      Except patting the backside of time
      you can't do anything
      neither planting the saplings
      nor cultivating,
      neither watering the plants
      nor yielding the fruits !

If your wishes are shattered
your desire and aspiration
would mingle in the flow of time.
Unknowingly your lazy hands
would be touching the pointed prickles
of the rose plant.
All those beautiful sceneries
become invisible.
All the fine tunes of music
become harsh and inaudible.

Dreadful comets fall
from the azure sky.
Explosive eruption of burning lava
from the volcano occurs.
The tone of cuckoo cracks.
A galaxy of hidden memories
flow in the stream of river.

> All are games of time,
> some are dazzling with damsels,
> some are gloomy with darkness.
> We all are wooden statues
> in his invisible hands.

●

Inexpressible Time

I've no time
to express the time!

>Still, I'll have to find time
>to express it
>but I've no mathematical formula
>to measure its length and breadth,
>circumference, area, diameter,
>radius and how to draw
>its geometrical diagram!
>Is it spherical, triangular,
>trapezium, quadrilateral
>or an invisible, unthinkable
>portrait of infinite arms !

To express the time
I took water, air, soil, fire
and the sky as the
experimental materials
along with place, pulse and prudence.
Experimentation after experimentation
with new innovative techniques

each time,
but at mid-night I return
tired, exhausted,
empty handed.
A ray of success peeps
through the dim light of glowworms
in the dark night
in the distant horizon.
With new vigour and excitement,
next day, I become engrossed,
in the laboratory for a new discovery:
the explosion of time.

> But alas, all in vain !
> All the innumerable experiments
> for years, for centuries, for *yugas*
> become fruitless.
> Still the time
> is inexpressible,
> extremely inexpressible.
> At last I raised my hands
> upwards !

●

The Labyrinth of Illusion

Dead is that reptile,
but is an elixir for some organisms.
Rows of ants run towards it,
a game of prey and predator.
In this vicious circle
one day a predator becomes a prey,
all its strength and vigour
become shattered !

      Nirmâlya* may be obtained from the hell
      Bitterness of hell may be experienced
      in the heaven.
      This earth may be a hell
      for somebody,
      heaven for some others.
      According to the deeds
      one may suffer or enjoy,
      taste the taste of time
      with fruits of elixir
      or fruits of poison.

Lotus of virtue has bloomed
in the mud of sin.
In the heaven of virtue
enhance the pages of sin
the wayward top leaders of the society,
not caring for virtue or sin!

>   Really it is very difficult here
>   to tackle the vicious circle,
>   the *Chakravyuha* (labyrinth) of illusion.

●

*Nirmâlya : the dried Mahaprasad (cooked rice after offering to goddess Bimala) of lord Jagannath temple, Puri.

In the Quicksand of Time

When my father was there
he was performing all deeds,
tolerating all pros and cons,
facing all adverse situations,
lifting upwards the mountain of pathos and agony
with a finger like *Krishna*.

>There was no electricity in the village
>during my childhood.
>We used to sleep over wooden cots
>with mosquito nets in the courtyard
>during summer days.
>My father was fanning us with hand fan,
>mother was sprinkling water
>over mosquito nets,
>and we couldn't feel the rage
>of summer.
>But now we feel it very much,
>even though we spend our time
>in air-conditioned rooms,
>malls and offices.

Very much tasty
were all food items
prepared by my mother during my childhood
like mixed curry, whole brinjal fry,
whole mango pickle, Badichura*
Arishâ, Kâkarâ, Malpuâ, Kânti,
Chakuli, Mandâ, salty and sweet badâ
which I can't forget.

>All are now dreams today;
>those have been swept
>in the passage of time.
>In a wretched boat
>we are sitting now,
>visualizing the earth
>very faintly, dimly, sparsely.
>Where has gone
>the beauty of the nature !
>Bewildered we are.
>In the quicksand of time
>we all are metamorphosed
>each into an invisible dot !

●

* Badichura: An Odia recipe prepared from sundried lential (black gram).

As Father was There

As father was there
we couldn't feel
any fear or danger.
Everything was performed smoothly
without any storm or thunder.

      If any imperilment
      shows its face through the window,
      father could easily made him
      understand so that he couldn't
      dare to show his face next time.
      We, the children, were playing
      merrily in our protected courtyard
      or over the rooftop,
      catching the dragonflies
      which were flying like helicopters
      in our backside courtyard,
      fetching honey from the honeybees,
      multicolours from the butterflies
      listening to the sweet songs of the cuckoo.

As father was there,
I could learn from him

the difficult English words and grammar,
the tough formulae of Algebra
the explanation of Odia literature
and what not!
In leisure, I was reading
his heart touching poetry collection:
'*Jibana Marana Sakhâ*'
(companion of life and death).

>As father was there
>we felt the world as a merry land.
>Days were passing
>like easy arithmetic.
>Couldn't know how our
>school and college days passed swiftly
>in the passage of time.
>During the end of my service career,
>all of a sudden passed away my father,
>cremated him at *Swargadwara* of Puri.
>We were flooded wtih tears of pathos and
>despair.
>In rituals, all the hairs were
>shaven from my head;
>vanished all my aspirations and passions.
>Now I feel a vacuum around me.
>Alas! my father is not there to repel it
>to an unknown kingdom.

●

My Father's Shirt

Had been to my village today.
Opened the lock of my father's room.
Here and there were spider webs,
cleaned them.
Still hanging alone in the rack
the cotton white half shirt
of my father which he used to wear
for protection of heat in summer.
He was facing boldly
any small or big problem
in his lifetime,
just like the magic of a magician !

    Caressed a little that shirt;
    searching his pocket,
    one would get a piece of paper
    with a list of groceries
    to be bought from the
    shop of Ram Patra,
    list of vegetables to be
    fetched from the market.
    Mother would have told him:

Oh, have you remembered
to bring medicine for the
ailing younger son
suffering from fever since four days !
Gone are those days !

Father would be telling :
Children will take this year
honey and Chyawanprash
in the evening in winter.
Cough and cold willn't dare
to come anymore !
During examination of the children,
father used to advise to take
a spoonful of Phosfomin
along with a half cup of water.

All are now memorable rainbows
in the sky of the past.
The camphor has been evaporated
leaving aside only
the while half shirt of my father.

●

In the Aspired Point

It has been raining cats and dogs
in the deep dark night
time and again.
He has been drenched by rain,
thrilled and lost in the heart of
the sparkling lightning,
in the roaring thunderstorm
quivering the ear drum.

      Worshipping in the temple
      with incense sticks, earthen lamps,
      sandal paste, burning camphor
      he has been meshmerized
      with *mantra*, *tantra* and *yantra*.
      A divine aura has been emitting
      from the third eye
      in one unknown point of the time.
      He has been running day and night
      in search of the point of origin
      of that aura,
      running and running
      though wounded his hands and legs.

Again, floating forward
over the deep sea water
holding a wooden log.

En route, he has been fighting
with the shark, blue whale,
facing unthinkable, unbelievable
undescribable circumstances,
oozing out of blood and tears from his body.
When will he reach
his long aspired point ?

The Life

Life is like a water bubble.
Water and air are needed
for life to sustain.
From the auricle and ventricle of heart
flowing streams of blue and red blood
with murmuring sound
with a continuous speed
from birth to death.
Think a while
isn't it a miracle !

    Life exists
    in the bone and flesh
    adorned with the cloth of skin.
    Still, one crosses daily
    forbidden lines,
    not caring anybody.
    Trying to ascend the *Indrapuri*
    of heaven from the earth,
    or may fall down to hell
    or being kicked out by *Indra*

may stay in the middle
as a *Trishanku**
albeit with his head downwards
for all time to come.

But for a mere water bubble
is there plenty of time
to visualize dream after dream of fondness
whose pre and post states
are full of voidness !

•

*Trishanku: - a king of Suryavamsha, father of Harishchandra, described in the epic Ramayana, who was prevented by Indra from ascending to heaven in physical form. Indra angrily kicked him hurtling towards earth. But sage Vishvamitra was able to halt him midway by his ascetic power and created a new Swarga there. Later Indra relented and carried Trishanku to real Swarga on his own golden *vimâna*.

Tranquility

When I'm in voidness
lost in mahâsûnya,
the great voidness.
When I'm in full perfection
enveloped the entire earth.

    When pierced by prickles,
    the petals of red rose
    laugh like the laughing of Mona Lisa
    or cry like the faint crying of
    Mona Lisa ?
    When sandstorm occurs in oasis
    does the nightingale cry sobbingly
    or sing romantic songs
    thrilling the hearts of
    the cacti and date palms,
    which were lustreless covered with dusts.

When the moon appears in the sky,
the blue lily
unveils the veil from her face
to visualize thousands of blue dreams.

Can she see the black spot
on the moon which may speak
a lot of stories?
All the errors may be converted
to correctness in the white blood
of white carpet.
Peacefully sleeps the blue lily
in deep slumber
under the thrilled moonlight
in fulfilment.
In that state, she ascends tranquility
forgetting all her agonies.

The Battle

If a day would be
of forty hours instead of
twenty-four hours,
I would build a Taj Mahal
of my dream on the bank of
river Mahanadi
where a battle is now continuing
between the Kauravas and Pandavas.

    Without battle
    no one is agreeable
    to give even a drop of water;
    no one is ready to sacrifice
    one's own arrogance.
    All are eager
    to keep their pride
    at high esteem,
    trying to pull the invisible legs
    by their visible hands
    that stretch up to the sky.
    Dreadful sounds
    are congregating

      to enhance the dreadfulness.
      A cloud of uncertainty prevails
      in the faces of the common men.

Appealing before *Chitragupta**
to meet Yamraj to request him
to offer death-boon
to the arrogant rascals
of the upper side of the river.
Then only the terrified minds
of the lower side of the river
will sleep peacefully
dreaming to build
a new Taj Mahal.

•

**Chitragupta* : A Hindu deity who serves as the registrar of the dead. He is assigned with the task of maintaining the records of the actions of human beings in a register.

The Soul

In this life
we are husband and wife.

    In the next life
    I may be your wife
    and you, my husband.
    In this life
    we have taken birth as Hindus,
    in future lives,
    may take birth
    as Muslims or Christians or Sikhs
    or Buddhists or even
    as Jews !

Even we may take birth,
in our future lives,
in Russia or Japan,
America or Alaska,
Indonesia or Africa.
May be in this planet earth
or in some other planet having life

and if our souls would travel to
that planet in space,
inhabitants of that planet
may be extremely intelligent, strong
with fame and pride;
jealousy, envy, lie, resentment
may be zero in them.

> Like this, we may take birth
> generation after generation
> as our souls are above
> gender, caste and creed,
> place, time and person.

●

Thoughts of Corona – 1

Wearing trouser and punjabi
I'm going to the vegetable market.

      To get rid of unexpected invasion,
      tied my face with mask.
      To procure green fresh vegetables
      plucked by far off farmers,
      not caring any untoward incident,
      or else how will they thrive !
      But the vegetable market is blank,
      as if congregation and rush
      have taken shelter
      in the unreachable caves
      of distant mountain !
      Very less people
      are standing farther apart,
      a kilometre away
      or at a distance of six feet
      or is it not visible at all !
      With peculiar pattern
      their eyes are seen,
      admixture of happiness and fearfulness.

A long whistle is heard from the
distant horizon along with
a whipping sound.
Like madmen
the horses are running criss-cross,
putting their hooves
on sands or stones
muds or grooves.
With terrified groaning
are falling down fallacious crowns
of false vanity and extreme arrogance.
Not caring the sun or moon,
heavily penalized compulsorily
for their act of nuisance;
blood clots on the edge of sword.

    Heartlessness has been vaporized
    from the heart
    into some distant corners of the clean sky.
    The mother earth is now
    respiring peacefully
    and with splendid grandeur
    sleeping calmly and quietly
    on the fresh green carpet
    without any anxiety and tension,
    dreaming the dreams
    which she hadn't dreamt
    for centuries.

●

Thoughts of Corona - 2

Life and love are now false,
death is the real truth.
Invisible, untouchable and unthinkable
is now that death
without near and dear ones,
only for a mere smallest of the small virus,
a dreadful messenger of death.

> Perturbed now the entire earth,
> no country is left alone.
> The arrogant people,
> not caring the sun and moon,
> reigning over the entire earth,
> for months, years and centuries
> proclaiming themselves
> as the second god,
> are now shattered, perished
> mingled in the five elements of earth !

The entire earth is now peaceful,
noiseless, calm and quiet.
The animals are trespassing easily

over the man-made roads.
In the tender breeze
trees are oscillating merrily;
with excitement the clouds
are playing hide and seek
with the dazzling moon;
the moon seems to be in
full contentment amidst
the moonlit sky.

    The 'greenhouse effect'
    has diminished.
    Cooler now is the earth
    smiling serenely
    breathing comfortably.
    The sea water is now
    more blue and pacific.
    Treasure of beauty
    are the rivers and rivulets;
    clear and clean are the lakes;
    fishes are playing gleefully
    in the transparent water.

The Ganges is now laughing
to her heart's content,
which many a project
couldn't perform for years together
can now be easily accomplished
by the miracle of a mere corona virus !

Thoughts of Corona – 3

Pregnant desires
are now dead.
Pale presentations
adore now the cadavers.
Frightful fears
are now capturing
the entire kingdom.

    Golden dreams
    are now dreams of pathos.
    Dreadful darkness
    is now in daylight.
    Throughout the roads
    are now marching swords.
    Close the doors and windows
    ten by ten,
    lest they may enter
    getting the least opportunity.
    No mercy, nothing else.
    That dazzling fine edges
    would easily cut you into pieces
    and throw here and there,

wouldn't allow a moment
for bleeding of the blood,
so cruel, so brutal !

Senseless are now the vehicles,
lying paralysed in some remote
deadly deserts, thrown away
by the hot horrible sandstorms.
Devoteless are now
all the festivals of Lord Jagannath,
still are flying in the sky
the flags of different gods.

Terrible trepidation
in the market places, malls
parks and paths.
Wearing masks
are flag marching
all obedient soldiers.
If death comes by sudden
invasion of the enemy,
they would be martyrs,
flowers would be offered
over their cadavers with gun salute.
Will their near and dear ones
be satisfied by these acts ?

●

Thoughts of Corona – 4

One may appear in different roles
in different attires
as a son or a husband,
as a brother or a father
may be as a daughter or a wife,
as a sister or a mother
or even as a warrior of corona,
in various stages of the world.
After completion of the roles
all will return to their
invisible world.
One's last time
may be without near and dear ones,
without friends and well-wishers.
May not get an opportunity
to receive even a piece of bone
to perform rituals at *Swargadwâra*.

>From where did come
this miserable time
which also appeared
in this world

around hundred years ago !
People also used masks
during that time.
Alas! lakhs and lakhs of people
met their tragic end.

Now again it has
showed its face in a different version,
threating terribly the entire world.
Not sparing any body,
even if it may be an innocent child,
a young man, an old lady,
a helpless destitute
or a physically handicapped person.
Has no mercy at all,
invades the lungs of the sufferers,
he who is fortunate
may survive or
may enter the other world.

These are its unforeseen plays,
bestowed upon by god
as boon,
being furious by the reckless act
of arrogant modern men.
When will be the wound healed?

A Poem on Corona

You can see it
only through high power microscope,
not through the naked eye.

      It is a living entity
      if stays inside an organism,
      non-living object if stays
      in the soil, sand or pebbles.
      Indeed, a link between
      the living and non-living !

During the process of evolution
whether it had evolved first
or later is of controversy.
Extremely minute is it
called a virus.

      A virus is very simple
      in composition,
      consisting only of nucleic acid inside
      and protein coat around
      or may have an extra outer fat layer.

Thread like is the nucleic acid
having two types:
DNA or RNA;
even the virus may contain enzymes.
Some viruses have DNA
like smallpox virus,
or have RNA like AIDS
or Corona virus.
Prime cause of the viral disease
is the DNA or RNA.

Designedly built the corona virus
with two RNA threads,
two enzymes and
a protein coat around
over which is a fat layer,
the structure like that
of a Kadamba flower !

Smallest of the small
a mere virus
that has marred the entire universe.
Crores of people
have been affected,
lakhs of people have met
their tragic end.

Not satisfied,
still that tiny creature
is continuing its invasion.
Of course, time will come

the virus will be defeated
by the new weapons of man.

    Proclaimed the Japanese scientists:
    By genetic engineering
    the corona virus has been created
    in China.
    United all the human beings of the earth
    to be crowned with success
    in the dreadful corona war.
    And ultimately they won.

•

Have Come Alone, Will Go Alone

Corona virus is like a thorn apple
with thorn like structures outside,
but filled with poison
in its heart.

> With its pointed nails
> will pierce you, wound you
> and blood would ooze out.
> Easily will paste blue poison
> in the inner chambers
> of your lungs.

You'll be filled
with gloomy darkness,
suffer from terrible agony,
will run here and there directionless,
and may fall into a death well.
No body would be there
near you to give solace,
to take your bone
for immersion in the
holy water of the Ganges.

Just like you've come alone
like that you'll go alone,
leaving aside your
kith and kin alone.

One day all will forget that
in this world
there was an emperor known as
Alexandar the great
whose both the hands
were hanging empty
in both sides of his corpse
during the funeral cortege.

●

White Screen

Death follows birth,
birth ultimately meets death.
Life is a bridge
between birth and death.

    Life is a ludo board,
    sometimes climbing up in the ladder,
    next time may fall below
    in the mouth of a snake.
    Like studying arithmetic in the school,
    an ant climbs an oily pole
    ten inches per minute
    but falls below five inches
    in the next minute.
    Not predictable how much time
    will it take to reach the
    ultimate goal in the life !
    May be there severe storm
    that would flown away the pole
    leaving no sign of the ants.
    What to solve the problem of arithmetic ?

In the hands of time
life is a toy,
may compel you to dance many times
on the invisible stage.
Sometimes may make you laugh so much that
tears will roll down from your eyes.
Even will make you cry and cry
and ultimately may take you
from the audience
pulling a white screen.

●

Down Memory Lane

How fast elapsed
around half a century
in this world,
in India, in Odisha
in Bhubaneswar and at our
dear B.J.B College !

    At that time wearing half pant
    and half shirt we used to attend
    the pre-university classes.
    Lalit Panda, the topper of Odisha,
    also wore half pant,
    now in heaven.
    After completion of a period
    we used to run to another classroom.
    While we were sitting inside,
    the girl students were waiting outside
    till a lecturer comes.
    But now reverse is the trend.
    Even the principal (late Shiv Kumar Panda)
    was teaching us mathematics,
    making us to understand clearly
    difficult theorems.
    Pravat sir was elaborating us
    the reactions of acids and bases.

Satya Shankar sir was dramatically
reciting the 'The Highway Man.'
We were amazed by the teaching
of Chandrasekhar Rath,
D.K. Ssmantaray and others.

Used to read during holidays
the poetry collection '*Atmanepadi*'
of our English teacher
Soubhagya Kumar Mishra.
But now in the campus
is not laughing *Krushnachudâ* of those days.
In the cruel wind of the time
has been lost her colourful anchal.

Today we feel nostalgic
our sweet college days,
picnic at Nandankanan,
merriment and jungle feast
near Narayani temple of Bânapur,
college sports, drama, annual functions,
competitions, aspirations for receiving prizes.
Hidden in the invisible hands of time
all such memorable events.

After germination,
if a seed becomes a tree,
will it germinate again ?
But we wish
lest our college days
be come again !

●

Eternal Dazzling Star

Your life had made elegant
half a century of Odisha
in between nineteenth and twentieth century.
The flaming torch of your ideals
had enlightened
the nook and corners of Utkal.

> In this state
> there is no parallel
> to your sacrifices.
> You are the only
> shining light house
> of the sea of Odisha history.
> Without you
> the birth of a separate
> Odisha state would have been impossible.
> You are a miracle
> of the entire Odias !

Oh, the main architect of *Bakulbana* !
Oh, the frontliner of Odia education!

Oh, the crown of
truth, justice, law,
rules and regulations !
Oh, the saviour of
the destitutes and sufferers !
You are the only jewel
of Utkal.

> You were the excellent guide
> of store of knowledge,
> the emperor in the kingdom of poems.
> Longing now '*Dharmapada,*'
> spreading the arena '*Kârâkabitâ*'
> from land to sky.
> Echoing now in every mind
> '*Bandira Atmakathâ*'
> '*Upâkhyâna Nachikhetâ*',
> but how many are now
> thinking positively
> '*Abakâsha Chintâ*'.

You are an eternal dazzling star
in the sky of Utkal.
Millions of salutes and
bows down before you.
Oh, immortal Gopabandhu Dash !

The Last Breath

In disturbed mind
sometimes question arises:
When a man dies
does he die by taking
the last inhale
or leaving the last exhale?
Although we know that
a man dies with the last breath
of exhaling.

>If blood of greed and attachment
>flows in the arteries and veins
>of a person, he'll wish
>to take the last breath as inhale
>to make more deep
>the redness of his blood
>by mixing oxygen.
>But alas,
>at that time
>his blood would have been watery !

But if blood of truth and justice
flows, then he'll wish
to leave the last breath as exhale
to give out to the earth
her air that he has burrowed
from her in his lifetime
time and again.
There is no value now
to keep that air
in his crumpled lungs
where there is not even an inch of space?

    Hence, I prayed:
    Oh God !
    Let my last breath
    be an exhale.

•

PUBLISHED BOOKS OF THIS AUTHOR

I. LITERARY BOOKS
Odia Poetry Collections
1. 'Shâdhee', Unique Publishers, Cuttack, 2002.
2. 'Andhârare Indradhanu', Anwesana Prakashani, Bhubaneswar, 2007.
3. 'Nasta Nakhyatra', Sudhanya Prakashani, Bhubaneswar, 2013.
4. 'Sabdamânanku Nei Swapna', Kahani, Cuttack, 2014.
5. 'Adrushya Chitrapata', Anwesana Prakashani, Bhubaneswar, 2015.
6. 'Panjurira Prajâpati', Publishing House, Bhubaneswar, 2017.
7. 'Nishabda Banshiswana', Black Eagle Books, USA, First International Edition, 2021.

English Poetry Transcreations
8. 'The Rainbow in Darkness', SSDN Publishers and Distributers, New Delhi, 2014.
9. 'The Butterfly of the Cage', Black Eagle Books, USA, First International Edition, 2023.
10. 'The Silent Flute', Black Eagle Books, USA, First International Edition, 2024.

Hindi Poetry
11. 'Nishabda Banshiswana' (Translated by Dr. Ajit Prasad Mahapatra), Authors Press, New Delhi, 2024.

Short Story Collection
12. 'Marichikâre Manishatia', New Age, Balasore, 2000.

Popular Science Collections
13. 'Upakari Udvida', Dibyaduta Prakashani, Cuttack, 2003.
14. 'Udvidamânanka Madhyare Ghrunâ O Prema', Jagannath Rath, Cuttack, 2012.

15. 'Jin Bigyânara Jayajatrâ', Gyanajuga Publication, Bhubaneswar, 2014 (recipient of Odisha Bigyana Academy Award, 2015, Rajadhani Book Fair Award, 2014, and Kalinga Book Fair Award, 2016).
16. 'Mânaba Sebâre Udvida', Gyana Bigyanika, Cuttack, 2015 (Bhubaneswar Book Fair Award, 2017).
17. 'Bigyânara Darpanare Aji', Shakti Publishers, Cuttack, 2016.
18. 'Phala Khaibâ Sustha Rahibâ', Gyanajuga Publication, Bhubaneswar, 2023.
19. 'Bhâratara Chandra Abhijâna', Gyanajuga Publication, Bhubaneswar, 2023.

Scientific Novel

20. 'Mangala Pathe', Kitab Bhawan, Bhubaneswar, 2019

General Knowledge

21. 'Ajira Dibasa', Shakti Publishers, Cuttack, 2016

Editing Poetry Anthology

22. 'Jibana Marana Sakhâ', by Late Harihar Sahu, Gyanajuga Publication, Bhubaneswar, 2014.

II. SCIENCE TEXTBOOKS

Apart from the above literary books, Prof. Sahu has 36 science textbooks for secondary, higher secondary (CBSE/NCERT/ISC) and degree (CBCS) classes at state and national level. The science textbooks at degree level mainly include biological sciences like Plant Physiology, Plant Metabolism, Plant Biotechnology, Plant Ecology and Phytogeography, Biomolecules and Cell Biology, Molecular Biology (both for Botany and Zoology Honours), Genetics, Plant Breeding, Natural Resource Management, Microbial Physiology and Biochemistry etc.

Thus, he has in total 58 books to his credit uptill now.

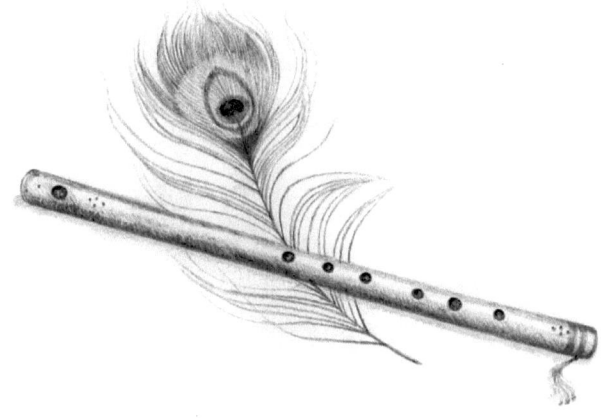

BLACK EAGLE BOOKS

www.blackeaglebooks.org
info@blackeaglebooks.org

Black Eagle Books, an independent publisher, was founded as a nonprofit organization in April, 2019. It is our mission to connect and engage the Indian diaspora and the world at large with the best of works of world literature published on a collaborative platform, with special emphasis on foregrounding Contemporary Classics and New Writing.

www.ingramcontent.com/pod-product-compliance
Lightning Source LLC
Chambersburg PA
CBHW060613080526
44585CB00013B/807